METAPHORM

Pamela Turton-Collens

© 2009 Pamela Turton-Collens
All rights reserved.
ISBN : 978-1-4092-8506-9

A Powerful 10-Part Process for Creating Your Happy Life-Story

About the Author

The author is a highly experienced teacher and trainer, having worked with children, young people, adults and professionals in all aspects of education, healthy lifestyles and personal, social and health education, including training professionals to use NLP based tools to promote positive change. The approach is creative and innovative, making use of her experience and skills to produce and deliver materials and programmes which are engaging and suited to the different needs and learning styles of the participants.

Pamela has a Master's degree in Language, Arts and Education, has trained in Brief Solution Focussed Therapy, holds a certificate in Counselling Skills in the Development of Learning and is a Certified Practitioner of both Neuro-Linguistic Programming and Emotional Freedom Techniques.The Metaphorm programme was created by the author and is a unique, holistic approach, incorporating elements of life-coaching strategies, NLP, EFT and current thinking in applied positive psychology. The title, Metaphorm, is made up from some of these elements:

'Meta' refers to a higher level of learning, where we can bring about change easily and naturally when we deal with our core beliefs and values.
'Metaphor' is about the way we represent our experience and the 'stories' we tell ourselves. When we create a new metaphor for ourselves, it is a powerful way of accessing our unconscious mind and activating change, usually at an unconscious level.
'Metaphorm' is also a play on the word 'metamorph', introducing the idea of something transformed.

You can hear more about NLP, EFT and the Metaphorm programme with details of online programmes and holiday packages.
which will guide you towards your Happy Story.

See www.breakthroughbreaks.com .

CONTENTS

1. VISION

Begin With The Happy Ending
Understand The Meaning Of Your Metaphors and Use Them To Change Your Life

2. CHANGE

The Process of Change

3. ATTRACTION

What You Think and Feel About Most Are The Things You Bring Most of Into Your Life
The Pulling Power of The Feel-Good Factor In Your Life

4. BELIEF

How We Filter Our Experiences Through The Lens Of Our Beliefs
What Are Your Core Beliefs?
You Can Choose What To Believe About Yourself

5. AFFIRMATION

How Our Words Influence The Way We Create and Interpret Our Experience
The Impact of Self-Talk and Affirmations in Propelling You To Your Goals
Do You Give Yourself Permission To Have What You Truly Desire?

6. VISUALISATION

Seeing is the Key To Being:Using Visualisation To Make Positive Changes and Achieve Your Goals

7. RE-FRAMING

You Are The Author Of Your Life-Story So You Can Re-write The Script

8. LETTING GO

Emotional Freedom Techniques

9. INNER CORE

Develop A Strong Inner C.O.R.E. of Conviction, Optimism, Resilience and Enthusiasm
Join The Pro's

10. OUTCOMES

'Good' Goals: Meaningful and Ecological Outcome
Your Happy Story: Create a Metaphor For The Life You Want

1
Vision

Begin With the Happy Ending. The Story So Far-Happy with yours?
Learn How To Be the Creator of Your Happy Life-Story.

Successful people start with a dream or an important goal and have a very clear vision of what they want. They are very good at keeping focussed on the end result of what they want to achieve, whilst taking the steps they need to get there. NLP (Neuro-linguistic-programming) is often called the psychology of excellence; it teaches people to model excellent behaviour because the insights, skills and techniques it embodies are the result of more than 30 years of studying the way high-achievers think, talk and behave. It is an ever-growing, dynamic field.

What do you really want?

Think of the best experience you have had in the past 6 months; what happened? who was there? what were you doing? where were you? why was it so special to you?
Think of the worst experience in the past 6 months. What made it feel so bad?
If you had a magic lamp, what would be your first 3 wishes?
If you won the lottery, what would be the first 3 things you would pay for?
Write down 3 things you really feel strongly about
If you had to go away suddenly for 6 months, what 3 things would you do first?
Imagine you could do whatever you wanted. What would you do?
If you had only 6 months left to live, what would you do?

These exercises will help you consider what is really important to you. When we understand our true values, what really matters to us, we can be much more focussed and motivated to achieve our goals.

What is the happy ending in your story?

Think of a time in the future when you are really living the way you want to live.
Get a picture in your mind of that ideal time.
Where are you? Who and what are around you? What are you doing?
Really focus on that picture to make it as bright and vivid as you can, put sounds in and really get into the feeling of how good it feels.

Now you are ready to start the plot and plan each chapter of your story.Your Metaphors:Understanding the Meaning Of Your Metaphors and How To Use Powerful Metaphors To Change Your Life.

Maybe you never really give much thought to metaphors; perhaps they are something your teacher mentioned when you were doing Creative Writing in class, or in a Literature lesson at High School? Often when we think about metaphors we think in terms of writers using them to make a piece of work more interesting or dramatic. In reality, when you think about it, the language we use, and I mean everyone's everyday language, is generally rich in metaphors. We are usually unaware of the pervasiveness of metaphor and not just in language used but also in the way we and others think and act. Newspapers and advertisements, more often than not, use metaphoric images, music and/or language to get an idea across more powerfully or to convince and persuade us to look and think about something in a certain way.

There is much to be learnt by reflecting on the metaphors which are particularly significant to us as individuals. You see, metaphors are the language of the unconscious mind; they are symbols which carry deep meaning for us. An important part of the work of the psychologist Carl Jung was about the significance of symbolic language or metaphor. We dream in metaphor, the images and dialogue of dreams are symbolic in their presentation and interpretation. Our concepts about everything are metaphorical, and the way we conceive things to be determines how we behave in every area of our lives.

What are the significant metaphors in your life-story? Find and reflect on your own hidden meanings:

Write a story. Spend 15-20 minutes writing a story about any animal, bird, insect or sea creature as the main character.
What's your favourite fairy tale, story or film from childhood

Who is your favourite pantomime character?
Who is your least favourite character?
List 5 of your favourite songs
Which films/TV programmes have you enjoyed/identified with most?
Who is your most memorable character in history?
What are the most significant events in history for you?
Which ancient god/goddess do you identify with most?
Who do you regard as a hero/heroine?
Are you attracted to, perhaps even collect objects of a certain type or with a similar motif?

Take time to reflect on what each of these metaphors symbolise for you, how they reflect how you see yourself and others and give meaning to the way you regard your life experiences.

By now you will be aware of and at least beginning to recognise certain themes and issues which relate to your life and which you are unconsciously expressing through the metaphors you are attracted to and use in your everyday life. You will find that the first story you wrote is really a story about you! And now you are aware of how unconscious metaphors function in your life, you can consciously choose metaphors which relate to the way you want you and your life to be

.Through the Keyhole: The External Metaphors In Your Surroundings And How They Influence Your LIfe

Do you remember the television programme, 'Through the Keyhole'? The catchphrase, spoken in a charming Bostonian accent, was "Who lives in a house like this?" I think it had an appealing allure of a combination of voyeurism, psychology and detective work as we were led round the homes of absent celebrities, and invited to piece together a character profile by looking at the environments they had created. It was great fun, and very revealing to observe the colours, furnishings, goods and chattels the stars surrounded themselves with. They really spoke volumes about character, lifestyle, pleasures, interests etc.

Your External Metaphors

Take a detached view of what you surround yourself with. Play 'Through the Keyhole' with your home. What does your home say about you? And is it saying what you want to be saying?

What do you want to attract into your life? Is there anything blocking or contradicting what you want? For example, if you are single and want to be in a relationship, do you have any pictures or ornaments which depict couples in a loving or romantic way? Do you have a space that is conducive to romance and 'couple-activities'? Are there any broken items or fittings which might represent metaphorically something that needs 'fixing' in your life, or unwanted things and clutter which gets in the way? This can be fun; when I began to think in this way about my home I realised it had been weighing on my mind to clear and throw out many items from my loft, which is full of stuff from my past. This seemed very significant to me at a time of breaking with the past in some ways and making a new start in life.

Feng Shui Metaphors

The ancient art of Feng Shui offers more sophisticated and detailed insight into the effects of our surroundings on what we manifest in our lives. It is a complex discipline which uses characteristics and metaphors from the natural world, and a system of analysing, creating and correcting the flow of energy or 'chi' in one's environment, in order to invite balance, harmony, prosperity, good relationships and well-being into our lives. Even if you know little about Feng Shui, you can make a good start by clearing your clutter, which is said to encourage the right flow of 'chi'. Also introduce colours, objects and materials from the natural world, ideally representing the elements of fire, earth, wind and water, such as a real fire or woodburner, candles, flowers, plants, pebbles, wood, bamboo and water features.

'Wish-Boards'

A really specific way of creating metaphors to attract what you want in your life is to paste pictures and items, which represent what you desire, on a board. Some people call this a 'Wish-board'. Pictures could include inspirational quotes, loving couples, people doing what you want to be doing, objects you want such as a car or something for the home or a cheque or bank statement showing the amount of money you want to make in a period of time. Then when you look at your 'Wish-board' each day imagine having or doing whatever it is you want, as if it is happening to you now, in the present moment and really focus until you can feel the sensations of experiencing what you want. When you get good at this, you can really feel the pleasurable emotions, without actually having achieved the experience yet! And when you become accomplished at seeing your outcome in your mind, what you visualise will eventually materialise in your life.

2
Change

How You Can Change Through a 4 Part Process and Live the Life You Desire

How we change: Processes

There are 4 important processes involved in making changes in our behaviour:

Deciding
Motivating
Doing
Maintaining

1. Deciding

First you need to decide what it is you want to bring into your life story, and really see yourself doing and enjoying those things. Imagine writing your autobiography near the end of your life. Reflect on what you would like people to read about you. What would you and the main characters be doing and saying in your story? Think about every area and aspect of your life: Love and Relationships; Health; Achievements; Activities; Home; Work; Money.

2. Motivating

The motivation to change, the wanting, has to be strong enough to force you out of what is comfortable and familiar, even if is no good for you and not what you really want. Your ego will fight back to keep you where you are, because that may feel safer than stepping into new territory. So, part of our motivation comes from wanting to be rid of negative feelings, such as fear, anxiety, frustration, depression, hopelessness, loneliness, boredom etc. etc. It does not matter so much what the actual feeling is, just that it causes us pain and provides the **push,** the 'away from' motivation.

What is in your story now that is not really worthy of you, because it does not fit in with the life you want and can have?

What is spoiling your story?
What needs to go?
What do you want to delete?
What needs to change?

What will happen when you remove those blocks, habits, people, circumstances etc. from your life? What needs to be done to eliminate the unwanted stuff? Any pain you feel at this stage is going to really help you understand what it is that you want to move away from. Because what you really want to do is to feel good, don't you?

Whatever it is that makes you **feel good** is going to give you an even more powerful drive **towards** what it is you want in your life. Positive feelings are much more powerful and effective than negative ones, so you need to really focus on how good it will feel to be living the way you want to. Create the **pull of attraction** to those elements which make you feel happy. Say 'yes' to the vision or dream, 'no' to the things that get in the way.

3. Doing

Once you have decided what it is you really want, and the motivational drive towards it, and away from what you want to reject, is there, you are read to re-write your story.

The **Plot** or the Plan: what is going to happen?
Think of Setting (places)
Characters(people)
Dialogue (how are you and others talking?)
Action (what are you and your main characters doing?)
Consequences (what are the outcomes of all this?)

How are you going to do it? What are the goals, targets, steps, resources, knowledge and skills needed?

'**Inner Doing**': practise visualising, affirming, relaxing, perhaps meditating, to keep you focussed and in a resourceful state of mind.

'**Outer Doing**': take the first step towards; get the knowledge, skills and support you need from wherever you can. Begin from where you are now.

4. Maintaining

You will need to keep going until the changes you want have become a new feel-good part of life for you.

Practise the Inner and Outer Doing until they become habitual; enjoyable habits rather than something you have to do.
Celebrate everything that makes you feel good. Say a private thank you for everything you already have and everything that gives you pleasure which is coming your way.
Reinforce anything that feels good; note when, where and how it happens, and do more of it!
Think about what is working well. Are there any tweaks and changes that need to be made to the 'plot' to enable you to develop your Happy Story?

3
Attraction

What You Think and Feel About Most Are the Things You Bring Most of Into Your Life.

No matter who you are, how old you are or where or how you have lived so far, I am sure your life-story is a fascinating tapestry of moments, events, challenges, people and places.

Or think of your life as a movie - all the happenings, people, settings, sounds, dialogues, actions and outcomes and the feelings attached to these.

Is there a pattern to any of these experiences? Pay attention to any recurring themes in events, responses/reactions, people involved, dialogue (what was said/heard) and emotions experienced.

Consider what kind of a story you have been creating for yourself. If you could give your story a name what would it be?

What Story do you want?

You can create your own Happy Story, Love Story, Success Story or Whatever You Want Story by changing the way you think, speak and feel about your self and your experiences, past, present and future.

Bear in mind that if you keep writing, thinking and talking about negative experiences that's what the story will predominantly be about. The more attention you give to things the more you continue to attract them into your life. Einstein's definition of insanity is a favourite of mine. He said insanity was doing the same things over and over and hoping for a different result. So if we want a different result we need to change what we are doing.

Therefore, if you consistently think, write, talk about and visualise positive experiences and outcomes that's the story you are creating for yourself for the future - at this very moment.

Creating your story

Write about, talk to yourself about, think about, see your positive future…as if it is happening now
Pay attention to every detail. Hear the dialogue, the music; feel those uplifting emotions right through your body.
Affirm, visualise, rehearse the story you want in your mind.

The Pulling-Power Of The Feel-Good Factor In Your Life: How To Attract More Of What Is Really Pleasurable and Meaningful To You.

Think of a recent time when you felt really happy and content with life; really enjoying yourself.

Can you get a picture of the event to go with that?
Can you see what you are doing, where you are, who you are with?
Make your picture as vivid as you can, bright and colourful.
Are there any significant sounds, music, voices that you can hear when you recall the event?
As you recreate the event, notice how you are feeling; what is happening in your body.
Really savour the whole experience again.

It's a good idea to write about the event, making it as rich in descriptive detail as you can. Or make sketches which represent the event to you.

Think about what it was about that particular event which made you feel so good about yourself. Why did you choose that episode above others?
What is significant to you about the activity, people, place and the feelings you felt? Write some notes to help you remember. Now you have some valuable information about yourself and what you want to bring more of into your life.

Think it in the Mind - feel it in the Body

When you did this, did you notice how you actually could feel those positive feelings in your body? And do you know your mind (and body) cannot tell the difference between the original, actual event or the re-creation of it?

The physiological effects of feeling good have been investigated and recorded by scientists using today's sophisticated technology, showing that liftng your mood affects every cell in your body in a beneficial way. Positive energy and positive feelings are healing and lead you to create and attract more positive emotions, people, events and circumstances into your life. You have probably heard of the placebo effect of healing too, where patients have been given a pill with absolutely no medicinal benefits whatsoever and told that it would cure them. Because they believed that they would be cured, in some trials more 'placebo patients' recovered than those who were given actual medicine.

Whatever you can do to generate genuinely feel-good, happy sensations and thoughts will keep you positive, healthy and bring you more of the same. Smile, sing a song, listen to your some uplifting music, watch a funny film, evoke a happy memory, think of a baby, friend, loved one.

The Happy Habit

Research has found that happy people live longer. It has also been shown that people who express high levels of contentment with their lives are not that way because life has been easier, or because they are better-looking, slimmer, more intelligent or richer. It is because they are habitually happy; happiness is a habit to them! So, get into the habit of feeling good to feel good!

Please and Thank you

One really powerful way of feeling good and attracting the good things you want to have and happen in your life is adopting a habit of thankfulness for what you already have. For me sometimes it might be the beautiful sunrise or sunset, the wind on my face, a message from a loved one, the smile or antics of a child, the sight of a squirrel frolicking through the trees, a warm home on a cold day, catching a train on time, a meal enjoyed, a favourite piece of clothing worn. Anything - we all have something to be thankful for, and whatever we look for we will surely find, whether it makes us feel good or otherwise.

Think of something that you are thankful for.
Think of something that has made or makes you feel really good about
    yourself which you want to have more of in your life.
Say to yourself " I feel really good when..." and say what makes you feel

good.
Now say it in the present tense as if it is happening now: " I feel really good now that..."
Really picture it in your mind, and get into the feel-good sensation of it happening to you now

Imagine learning how to use exercises like these and many more skills, insights and techniques to really understand yourself, what you really want from life and how to get more joy from it.

4
Belief

Rose-Coloured Glasses, Or Just Dark, To Match Your Thoughts? How We Filter Our Experiences Through The Lens Of Our Beliefs

Our mind 'filters' information to match our beliefs in various ways. This serves a useful purpose as it makes the massive amount of sensory data we receive manageable, otherwise there would be literally too much information to 'take in' and make sense of. So, our mind makes sure that whatever we perceive is a match to whatever we believe. The problem arises with the unhelpful and/or limiting beliefs we hold, though to be aware of these mental processes can be really liberating and can actually be harnessed to assist us in reaching our goals.

Deletions:

The mind selects what we pay attention to, whilst ignoring other aspects. So, if you believe, for example, that blondes have more fun, you will tend to notice blondes enjoying themselves.

Distortions:

The incoming sensory data is adjusted to represent what is real in a different way. A clear example of this is seen in the completely distorted body-image of anorexics, who actually see themselves as physically fatter when they look in the mirror, rather like those 'Hall of Mirrors' at fairgrounds and science museums.

Generalisations:

This is where conclusions are drawn about people, things or circumstances based on a few experiences. This process is useful in collecting and analysing data, but can encourage us to form beliefs which get in the way of our fulfilment and happiness. An example of this would be if you and a few friends had all shared the experience of having a romantic partner who was unfaithful, which might lead you to conclude that most men, or women, cannot be trusted. Notice when you use the words 'always' in your speech or thoughts. Also 'never', 'all', 'none' are indicators of generalisations.

Beliefs

It is empowering to be aware of the beliefs we hold, because often when you take on beliefs about yourself, others, problems and circumstances, you are translating that which you desire, your wants, into needs, which express themselves as demands and expectations, thereby setting yourself and others up to fail, in your eyes, leading to disappointment and diminished sense of self-worth.

Choosing what to believe:

We are in charge of our beliefs, and can decide to choose those which will serve us well and be the foundation structure of our happiness. Deciding what we want to believe, and applying powerful processes, including affirmations and visualisations to support and replace unwanted beliefs, will put you in control of your life.

Decide what you want to believe
Affirm to yourself the new belief.
Write it down and repeat it to yourself frequently.
Get a picture in your mind of you in which you see yourself in a way that matches your new belief.

What Are Your Core Beliefs? They Are The Keys To Personal Development and Improvement

When we access and examine our core beliefs we are able to bring about more rapid positive change in our lives, as our beliefs about ourselves (and others) drive much of our behaviour.

The beliefs you hold about yourself can be very benevolent and motivating ones, for example you may believe that you are hard-working. Your unconscious mind will do its best to help you prove it by always applying yourself to any task you are faced with.

There are also beliefs which limit us and hold us back from behaving the way we really would like to be. Think of a habit or behaviour you dislike about yourself. e.g. I am untidy, not good in the morning, not good at exams etc. etc.

You may now be saying that surely these behaviours are about one's character and cannot be changed. True, a lot of our behaviour stems from our natural traits and tendencies; it's also true that a great deal of it is learnt behaviour. And in order to behave in a certain way, we have to believe that that is how we are.

So, for simplicity we will call our beliefs Limiting Beliefs and Empowering Beliefs. We will consider later how any beliefs can work in positive or restricting ways - we just need to be aware of how they are controlling our behaviour, and make them work for our and others' benefit. Beliefs in themselves are neutral, neither good or bad or even right or wrong; it is the effects they have on our behaviour which can be positive or negative, limiting or empowering

Limiting Beliefs

Think of something you dislike and want to change about yourself. For example you may believe that you have a tendency to be overweight and eat too much. Or are frightened of something to the point that it holds you back, such as fear of flying, commitment in a relationship or a phobia etc. Get a picture of yourself behaving that way. Notice the details in the picture, including any sounds, and any feelings in your body that come with it.

Empowering Beliefs

Now focus on something you like about yourself, enjoy doing and believe you are good at. Picture a time when you were doing that feel-good thing. Again notice what is going on in the picture, any sounds and feelings that accompany it.

When did you start to believe that?

Start with the limiting belief. If you could guess, when was the first time you believed that you behaved like that? Just go with the first memory, image, voice or feeling that comes up in response to that question. Do the same for the empowering belief you have about yourself, noticing details, sounds and feelings.

Swapping a 'bad' belief for a 'good' belief

Think of something you want to change
Get a picture or movie in your mind of being that way; focus on what is going on and the feelings that you experience
Now get a picture of a time when you were behaving or feeling in an opposite way. Focus on the details and feelings.
Click your fingers to clear your mind
Bring the first, limiting, picture back in your mind; focus until it is really vivid and strong
Now imagine you have a remote control to shrink that picture until it is very small
Click your fingers and quickly put the empowering picture on the screen in your mind
Turn up the colours, volume, feelings until it is bright, vibrant, loud and 'full-on felt' in your body
Have fun playing and practising this technique; start with something trivial and work up to more significant change.

Who Are The 'Who Said-So's' In Your Life? You Can Choose What to Believe About Yourself

When we consider how we came to hold certain beliefs about how we are, and identify with those beliefs, whether they are positive or negative, empowering or limiting, we can trace some of those to things people have said to us. We are often surprised, when we recall the said-so's in our life, that they might often have been people whom we regarded as having no real or lasting influence, or whose opinion we did not necessarily respect. Or it may be that something was said that already confirmed (in our minds - remember beliefs are not necessarily the truth - they are our created truths) a previously formed belief. And once we have taken on a belief about ourselves, we then filter what people say to us so we are only giving attention to anything which reinforces our belief, and disregarding anything which does not.

For example, how many of us know at least one beautiful-looking woman who firmly believes she is unattractive? Think of anorexics, an extreme case of a belief system which actually distorts the physical reality. Do you believe you are attractive, lovable, healthy, wealthy?

Who said so ?

What beliefs do you hold about yourself? Write down a few that come to mind and note anything someone once said about you that 'sticks in your mind'. Or start with things people have said about you that you recall vividly, and write down any thoughts you may have about how this may have caused you to believe something about yourself. It's usually revealing to begin with your parents and then think of close family, teachers, friends, peers at school, tutors, colleagues etc.

Self-image

Are there any particular words, phrase or descriptions either parent used more than once about you? If you have brothers and sisters it's an interesting exercise to ask them what their memorable quote is for each parent. I am one of a large family of eight, and was fascinated to learn that each of my siblings had a different remembered dialogue for each of my parents, which of course was significant only to them. My father, for example used to tell me that "I was more like him than he was". The speech I remember of my mother's, when I had done wrong, was that I "was just like my father", thus reinforcing a belief that I had inherited some of his undesirable characteristics, a belief it took many years to re-frame into a much more positive belief that I shared some of his enviable attributes, such as his intelligence and humour.

Other beliefs

Think about beliefs you think you hold about other areas of life such as money, marriage, sex, children, work etc. Was there a 'said-so' you recall when you think about those aspects.

Some examples I have heard are:

Money - rich people don't care about people like us (belief: you cannot be rich and compassionate)
Housework - women with clean houses are boring and have no lives
Marriage - you lose interest in sex after a few years
Having children - you can't do what you want after you have had children

You can probably come up with quite an entertaining list, So often, though, we take on these beliefs, particularly from our parents, without questioning the truth of them or even being aware that we are internalising them.

Metaphors

People frequently use metaphors in their dialogue which are very revealing about underlying beliefs because they reflect our concepts and perceptions.

Examples

Marriage isn't a bed of roses
Money doesn't grow on trees
She looks like mutton dressed as lamb
You are getting too big for your boots

The good news is that you can choose the dialogue you want to keep in your story. Simply re-write it. For example, if you believe you are unattractive, tell yourself how attractive you are. Give your self-talk a feel-good affirmation, such as "I really enjoy my attractiveness".
If you have negative beliefs about money, replace the said-so with something beneficial to you, such as "I always have plenty of money".
Think about what you want to bring into your life and write your own happy-story dialogue!

5
Affirmation

Watch Your Language! How Our Words Influence The Way We Create and Interpret Our Experiences

It is really important for our well-being and development that we become aware of the way we talk, our inner dialogue as well as the words we use to express ourselves to others. By noticing and taking control of our self-talk, we can direct our thoughts and feelings towards what we want to attract in our lives. Most people either do not give any thought to the words they habitually use, viewing them as automatic and inherent in some way, yet it is really empowering to learn that actually you can choose your self-talk and consequently how you feel, and be in charge of what happens to you.

Our unconscious minds are picture-orientated, servile to our thoughts and feelings, and will accept whatever we present to it as a picture. Our thoughts, and the words we use to express those thoughts, create a picture in our minds, with associated feelings in our bodies. Try thinking of something you don't like, and notice the words, the picture triggered in your mind, and the feelings you feel. Click your fingers to clear the picture, then do the same exercise, with thoughts of something you really like. Your unconscious mind cannot distinguish between what is really happening or just in your imagination.

So can you appreciate now how empowering it will be for you to visualise, think, feel and talk about what you want in your life, and take your attention away from those things you do not want. If you are constantly thinking about, picturing, talking, and thus feeling about negative behaviours, situations or circumstances, you are drawing more of the same into your life. By the same process, you attract more positive outcomes when you give your thought and energy to what is desired, when you find ways to cut off limiting and unhelpful self-talk and replace it with uplifting and affirmative words.

Affirmations

An affirmation is a declaration of belief. Our behaviour is controlled by beliefs we have about ourselves, the way we see ourselves and the thoughts, words and feelings which come with the pictures we hold in our minds.

If for example, you talk to yourself in ways like this:

"I've always found it hard to.."
"Things have never../I have never."

Statements like this will trap you in the same behaviour and conditions. People who overcome challenges and achieve their goals use positive affirmations, see themselves as successful and view failures as temporary setbacks, 'blips' or learning stages on the way to 'winning'. You can begin by 'catching' yourself
when your self-talk is getting in the way of your happiness, and use it to reverse it and convert it to an affirmation of the way you want things to be.

Such as:

"It is easy for me to.."
"I always.."
"I am../I enjoy../I deserve../I am happy and thankful that.."

Always state in the positive, and in the present tense, as if it is happening to you now. The unconscious mind does not process negatives, so instead of declaring "I enjoy not smoking" or whatever it is you want, affirm "I enjoy having more money/better health/ cleaner lungs/whiter teeth/ fresher breath" etc. Use words to describe the benefits which resonate most strongly with you, in order to generate the good feelings to reinforce the picture in your mind.

"**What you resist, persists.**" Carl Jung

Some other kinds of self-talk set up resistance within us and others, and help to perpetuate the things we do not want. Be aware of language which makes demands on you and others, such as "have to/got to/ must/ should/ ought to", which usually result in a resistance-response, for example, "I can't/won't/won't be able to/ I'll never/ Why should I? " It is essential to find the feel-good, 'wanting-to' place of whatever needs to be done to get you to your goal. You may not really enjoy cleaning, but if you focus on enjoying having clean, pleasant surroundings, you will attract the solution or find the motivation to achieve that. Focus on what it is you intend to enjoy, rather than your performance or behaviour.

Finally, one more word to throw out of your self-talk is 'try'. When you use the word, 'try', ask yourself if you either want to do the thing, have any intention of doing it, or really believe it is possible. Trying is not doing, so have a clear intention, use words which evoke positive thoughts, pictures and feelings within you and repeat them to yourself until it becomes a habit for you. Enjoy where you are now, and your results!

Say It Like You Want It, Not How It Is Right Now. The Impact Of Self-Talk and Affirmations In Propelling You To Your Goals

Research has shown that we create in our reality, in other words we move towards and eventually become that which we think about. Because our minds are picture-orientated, our thoughts evoke pictures and associated feelings which means that physically, emotionally and psychologically, our thoughts create our future conditions and experiences whether they are good for us or not, or even whether we wanted or intended them or not. Many people believe they have no control over their thoughts and feelings, and so do not believe they have to take responsibility for them and learn to be aware of them, if they are going to avoid attracting into their lives things that are not desirable, by default.

Therefore, it is really important to always be looking in the direction you want to be heading. Anyone who knows how to lead a horse knows it is important to do just that. The unconscious mind is servile to your thoughts, beliefs, values and feelings and accepts what you present to it as a picture, your 'script'.
Regularly thinking about what you do not want, or like, will create more of those undesirable habits, behaviours, people, events and circumstances .
Your unconscious mind does not process negatives. To understand this concept, experiment with it. Think about if someone tells you not to do or think about something, for example right now do not think about a tree. It is really hard not to think about a tree, isn't it? So, if you keep giving attention to what you do not want, you will be drawn towards it. It is vital that you keep your focus and energy directed on that which you do want to attract or create in your life, and withdraw any energy and attention, through thought and feeling, from that which you do not want.

Affirmations

In order to take control of your thoughts, and the mental pictures and body emotions you are generating through them, it is necessary to control your self-talk. Affirmations are a really effective way of doing this. By making a statement of belief about ourselves in keeping with what we want to create or how we want to be will reinforce a positive picture in our minds. To understand this better, become more aware of how other people around you talk about things and what usually happens to them, to gather some evidence for yourself about how the way we talk about things reinforces and creates experience.

For example, how many times have you heard statements like this:

"It's always been really hard for me to.."
"I've always been unlucky with.."
"Things have never come easy to me."
"I am hopeless at.."

All the negative self-talk needs to be shut off and turned around with positive affirmations, which become more effective the more frequently you repeat them. For instance, " I am hopeless at making time/money/decisions/friends"can be replaced with " It is easy for me to make time/money/decisions /friends" etc.

The more relaxed you are when making affirmations, and the more vividly you can create a mental picture and evoke strong feelings to accompany them, the more real, compelling and powerful they will be in driving you towards the future you want to see yourself living.

Permission:Do You Allow Yourself To Have The Things You Really Want In Your Life?

Ask yourself, "Do I give myself permission to..have a loving relationship, be slim, be well, have money, enjoy myself etc etc.?

Ask and be mindful of the answers that come back. If there is resistance, you need to explore where that is coming from, such as old beliefs you have about yourself, or unquestioned opinions and values which no longer serve you. Your ego wants, and will fight for you to stay in your comfort zone. Also be aware that others around you may be more comfortable keeping you as and where you are, and if you change, aspects of your relationship with anyone and anything will change too. And if your reasons for this change are good enough to compel you in this direction, then the change will be for the better. So, as you reflect on your answers, consider how you changing can ultimately benefit those around you.

For example:

If you felt resistance to the question about a loving relationship, are there things you like about being single which you feel you may forced to give up?
If you were thinner, are you frightened people around you may treat you differently?
Does being affluent worry you that your relationships might suffer or you would be less of a nice or good person, because somewhere you took on the belief that that was so?
If your career was successful, are there concerns that you would not be as good a mother or wife, husband or father, because you were brought up to think that way?
Would getting well mean that you are frightened you might get less attention and support, or be expected to do more?

To really get to the feeling place of how changes would improve your life, ask yourself what the change would bring to you until you get to a very clear, strong positive feeling about the change. This will help you bring about the change by making it more compelling, and build a stronger inner voice to motivate you.

For example, if I say to myself, "I want more money", then ask myself what that would bring to my life, the answer might be "financial security". If I then question what financial security means to me, it may mean the freedom to live and work anywhere in the world. And so on. Keep questioning with alert awareness of the feelings that accompany each answer until you hit the powerful source of the wanting. When you understand your unique, good reasons for wanting you will find it easier to give yourself permission to have whatever it is.

6
Visualisation

Seeing Is The Key To Being. Using Visualisation to Make Positive Changes To Get What You Want

Even if Kate Winslet has heard of, or knowingly uses Neuro-Linguistic Programming Techniques now, it is highly unlikely that she had any clue what they were at the age of eight. Yet, on receiving her coveted Oscar at the recent Awards, she described the powerful process of visualisation. She mentioned how, as an eight year old girl, she used to practise the speech she would make on accepting her Oscar, whilst looking in the mirror.

Similarly, in a recent magazine interview, the BBC Radio DJ, Scott Mills, talked about how, at the age of six, he used to pretend to be a DJ and put on a show for his mother and his teddy-bears. Daley Thompson, the Olympic athlete is reported to have said, when asked if he used Neuro-Linguistic-Programming techniques, that he did not, but then went on to discuss how he mentally rehearsed every stage of his performance from beginning to a winning end. In other words, he saw himself completing his course successfully, in every detail, as part of his preparation for competition. In other words, he visualised being a winner.

In an experiment conducted in the 1980's, referred to as Visual-Motor Rehearsal, Olympic athletes were wired up to sophisticated bio-feedback machinery and asked to visualise every aspect of their performance. Astonishingly, the results showed that their bodies responded as if they were actually performing; the heart-rate, blood pressure, the muscle response etc. all recorded as would be expected when the athletes were competing! This was because the mind cannot distinguish between a real or imagined event, which is why we can re-create the actual physical feelings when we think about something we feel strongly about.

So, visualisation is an incredible tool to help you achieve what you want. If you can see yourself doing and being in the way you want to be in the future, as if it was happening to you right now in the present, you can make that happen for yourself. So get mentally rehearsing, even if you feel silly accepting that desired award whilst talking to yourself in the in the mirror, or giving the performance of your life to your pets or teddy bears. Just think of Kate, Scott, Daley and many, many others who had the vision to achieve their goals, by achieving them in their imagination first.

Steps to Effective Visualisation:

Get a clear picture in your mind of what you will be doing when you achieve your goal.
Find a picture that creates the strongest emotional sensation in your body when you think about it. Write about it, draw it. Move through it if you can.
Make the picture, or movie, as vivid, clear, and colourful as you can.
Put in lots of detail. Surroundings, people, sounds, even smells - the more stimuli you can evoke, the better.
Practise doing this as often as you can. The more frequently you do it, the sooner you can achieve what you want.

7
Re-framing

Half Full or Half Empty? You Are The Author Of Your Life-Story So You Can Re-Write The Plot

Do you know you can choose the way you perceive your experiences? One of the presuppositions of Neuro-Linguistic-Programming (NLP), which is often called the psychology of excellence because it provides a model of what high-achievers do, is that there is no failure, only feedback. In other words, you can choose to regard anything which does not work out right for you or the way you wanted it to, as a learning step in finding the right way to go about it. Most successful people, if you do even a little research, have experienced setbacks, and even what others might consider to be spectacular failures. You will see that they learnt from their mistakes, made adjustments to the way they did things and had the faith and resilience to continue until they achieved success. I love hearing stories about people who were told, often when they were young, that they could not do something, that they lacked the abilities in some way, then went on to achieve remarkable results. There are many examples of this in the histories of famous people such as Einstein, Winston Churchill and so on. I had a friend who was consistently placed in the bottom grade for Mathematics at High School, and achieved a doctorate degree in quantum physics by the age of 30.

Re-Framing, PollyAnna and Playing The Glad Game

Re-framing is a technique used in NLP to change a negative perception of a person, situation or event into a positive one which allows you to be in a happier, more relaxed and therefore more resourceful state of mind. Think of Pollyanna, the cheerful girl in the book and the film, who always saw something good in everything. My sister has her own version, which she calls the 'Glad Game'. For everything that happens which might easily be perceived as negative and undesired, the Glad Game involves finding something useful or worthwhile about it. It can become a very enjoyable habit to acquire, which eventually will attract more positive people and situations to you. Even if at first you are not convinced of the advantages in a situation, have fun with it and notice how you can choose to shift your feelings about anything. It might also prove really irritating (i.e. uncomfortable) to people who are determined to cling onto their miserable viewpoint, so at times it may be better to play the Glad Game in the privacy of your own mind.

Play around with things which seem 'small' or quite trivial to begin with, if you are more comfortable with that, then apply it to things which seem 'big' to you, the really important stuff. Let's look at some examples:

You've missed your bus/train and are going to be late for work. You could re-frame that to decide that you enjoy being early and feel more motivated to make sure you are next time. Or it could just be that the next bus won't be as congested and you'll have a more comfortable ride. Maybe you didn't eat breakfast and it gives you chance to grab a tasty snack.

You go to Weight-Watchers and haven't lost anything at your weekly weigh-in. Perhaps that special occasion meal or party was worth it anyway, and you know that won't be happening next week. Or have you just made other 'non-losers' feel better?

You didn't get the job you really wanted? It's an opportunity to get useful feedback when you go after the job that is going to be really right for you. You may also have noticed things about your potential colleagues, journey to work and/or workspace that you would prefer to be different in your ideal job, anyway. Unsquashable optimism is an important part of this.

Your feelings can provide an excellent guide to this; for example, if you are feeling really wretched about the way someone has treated you, you can look at it as providing you with an indicator of the way you do want to be treated, and focus on how that would be and how good it would feel.
It can be also be really liberating to re-frame your past experiences this way, and free yourself from the cumbersome baggage you have been carrying around with you. You can let go of all those heavy thoughts of deprivation, neglect, rejection, disappointment, guilt, heartbreak, failure when you can find a way of looking at them from a different vantage point. You have control over the script of your life-story, so write, and re-write it, until it becomes your Happy Story. Enjoy!

8
Letting Go

Whenever You Feel Afraid Whistle A Happy Tune Or Try 'Tapping' and Neuro-Linguistic-Programming to Free You Of Irrational Feelings, Anxieties, Fears and Phobias

We all have something which triggers off a response we find hard to explain or understand in a rational way. It may be something relatively minor, in that it does not interfere with the general smooth-running of our lives. Or a much more dramatic reaction to a thing or set of conditions which is damaging and/or completely inhibiting in that it prevents us from doing or responding in the way we want to.

Irrational emotional responses can be triggered by words or phrases used by another, a tone of voice, gestures or body language, a certain type of person or set of circumstances or conditions, smells, sounds, visual stimuli such as objects and creatures and even our thoughts about these things. Because our unconscious mind does not know the difference between something that is actually happening and something we are just imagining is happening, either way it can produce the same emotions and physical feelings. Try this exercise to demonstrate how your mind does not distinguish between how an actual experience feels or a remembered one:

Think of a really exciting, maybe frightening, experience you had, perhaps at a funfair. Hold the picture in your mind , blow it up and make it as vivid as you can, with details such as sounds if you recall them. Can you feel the sensation of the experience?

Irrational emotions are described as such because usually we cannot explain why we feel like this, and are rooted in some past event which we have repressed and forgotten about, yet still hold the memory of in our unconscious, and in our physical bodies.

Emotional Freedom Techniques are a simple, gentle, yet really effective way of uncovering the layers of these trapped emotions, rather like peeling the skins of an onion and releasing the negative emotions and physical feelings which accompany them. It works by identifying the key events, emotions and physical responses and performing a series of tapping on the main acupressure points to release the blocked energy. With the release often people will sigh deeply or laugh (everyone has their own expression of release) and wonder how something could have affected them so strongly and for so long without them really understanding why. You do not need to understand how it works to benefit from it, like electricity or the internet!

Lost Baggage: Emotional Pain From The Past and How To Lose it.

Most people accept the idea that the majority of us carry around what is termed as 'emotional baggage'. This generally refers to any unresolved negative emotion from some event or incident in the past, which we are holding on to and have difficulty letting go of. Whenever we have a strong emotional or compulsive response to a thought, comment, person, set of circumstances or any external stimuli, such as a picture, sound or smell, which we cannot make sense of, we can be sure there is an unresolved emotion lurking. Or we may have a chronic condition, such as physical pain or feeling inexplicably 'low', perhaps triggered in certain situations.

It is always worth exploring and understanding why we have trouble letting go. Sometimes the problem may be that the issue is too painful to face. The unconscious mind represses painful memories which have unresolved negative emotion, and will re-present them for resolution until the feelings are acknowledged and rationalised.

Eckhart Tolle, in his recent book, 'A New Earth', describes what he calls the 'pain-body', which he sees as existing almost as a separate entity within us, and which he says is stronger in individuals who have experienced trauma, such as brutality, abuse or severe neglect. Tolle believes this 'pain-body' lies dormant until it needs to replenish itself by feeding on negative emotional energy.

However you view this trapped negative emotional energy, what is certain is that wherever it exists it prevents us from being in the full flow of life and well-being. The beauty of Emotional Freedom Techniques is that you do not need to understand what is causing your emotional imbalance, your bad habit, eating disorder, depression, phobia, poor health, low energy etc. etc. Acknowledging the body-sensation with the feeling, affirming your love and acceptance of yourself, and tapping on the acupressure points whilst acknowledging the feeling, will eventually release the block. Some blocks will clear miraculously in a session, others may be 'layered', like an onion skin, each 'layer' needing to be released, until the root emotional source, that is, the original incident which caused the pain, is cleared. A qualifed practitioner of Emotional Freedom Techniques can guide you through the process, which is a wonderfully simple yet powerfully effective way of freeing you of the past that holds you back from a fully enjoyable present and a compelling future.

Wiping Out Bad Memories:How Emotional Freedom Techniques Can Release Fearful, Traumatic and Painful Memories Without The Use of Drugs and Their Dangers.

Recent extract from Biology News:

"A single, specific memory has been wiped from the brains of rats, leaving other recollections intact.
The study adds to our understanding of how memories are made and altered in the brain, and could help to relieve sufferers of post-traumatic stress disorder (PTSD) of the fearful memories that disrupt their lives. The results are published in *Nature Neuroscience*"

This scientific breakthrough has been widely featured in the news recently. For me, it presents a real concern that memory is a highly complex neurological system which is connected to the physical body in ways which we do not yet fully understand, and so to chemically remove, if you like, painful memories from the brain, may not actually deal with the physiological memory. Emotional Freedom Techniques, on the other hand, also work on the painful feelings and psychological distress of traumatic and unhappy memories by releasing the energy-blocks of trapped emotions through tapping on the acu-pressure points of the body. You may not understand how it works, like electricity or technology, or even believe in it, yet it has proved to be a beautifully simple and astonishingly powerful method of releasing such emotions and restoring our minds and bodies to a state of equilibrium and ease.

Emotional Freedom therapy works on the principle that when we experience negative emotions, if the experience is not resolved and the energy released, it remains trapped, rather like a log in a stream, interrupting the flow of energy and a natural state of well-being. We know that the unconscious mind represses painful memories, which are re-presented in an attempt to resolve and release them, to restore psychological equilibrium. This is why we repeat behaviours until we can make these memories rational and let them go.

We all know how we can re-create, actually really feel as physical sensations, the body-feelings associated with painful memories. Try recalling an unpleasant experience now. Get a picture of it in your mind, and notice where you feel the discomfort in your body, perhaps a physical pain. There is usually a distinct feeling in an area of your body, which has its own characteristics, such as the quality of the sensation, (e.g. throb, tingle, ache, bubble, weight, sharp, dull, pulsating, static etc) size, shape, even texture and colour for some people. All of these characteristics can reveal to the Emotional Freedom Practitioner important information about the emotional experience, and are evoked at the outset of each session in order to release trapped, negative emotions and are used as a measure of intensity, by which the EFT therapist can calibrate the progress of the release, by the reduction of the intensity through each stage of tapping.

All psychological, emotional and physiological imbalances usually involve and can be traced to a connection with traumatic or unhappy experiences, whether it is illness, pain, irrational fears, emotions and phobias, compulsions and addictions and disorders or imbalances to do with food, such as over-eating, anorexia and bulimia. EFT is remarkably effective at getting to the root of these key experiences and releasing the energy blocks they create, thus freeing the individual from their terrible hold.

9
Inner CORE

Tough Going? The Tough Get Going By Developing A Strong Inner CORE: Conviction, Optimism, Resilience and Enthusiasm

C.O.R.E

Conviction

We do not allow ourselves to desire something we do not believe is within our reach. Decide what you truly want, ask yourself why it is so important for you to have it, until you get to the strong, inner, 'feeling' place of desire. Then develop a firm belief that you can have it and deserve it, the 'can-do' attitude. This may involve identifying any beliefs you might have which are blocking you from achieving what it is you want. Keep focussing on the end result, visualise and affirm it to yourself regularly until your inner voice is louder and more convincing to you than any on the outside, and your internal fire of desire is unable to be quashed by the damping doubters in your surroundings.

Optimism

Really practise optimism as a way of being. Even if you do not believe it at first, act and talk as if everything is happening perfectly, at the right time and in the best sequence to lead you to your heart's desire, until eventually you will realise the truth of it. Even though there may be people, experiences and events we would rather avoid at the time, trust that they are the experiences we need to go through to get to our goal, that our unconscious mind always knows what they are and will take us through them.
Look for and you will find the silver lining in every cloud and do not let it rain on your parade! Look for things to be thankful for and to get pleasure from, whatever your external circumstances are at the present moment.

Resilience

Think of the most awful experiences you have had, not to dwell on and relive the misery, but to remind yourself that you have actually survived, even learnt a lot, feel stronger and a better person for them, hopefully. Even just to have got through them is a demonstration of your resilience, which you can build up, rather like a muscle. A 'bounce back' muscle! Gather all the evidence of your resilience by re-playing all the positive steps you took to get out of and recover from any difficult experiences, and celebrate your ability to survive and grow in the face of adversity.

Enthusiastic Effort

When you are clear about what you want to create or achieve, imagine how good it will feel when you have achieved it. Ask yourself what it is you need to accomplish your goal. Where you are perceiving difficulties around having the skills or resources to do something, instead of saying 'I can't' or using any restricting language, say 'How can I?" (get the skills, money, support, resources etc) and see what answers come up for you. If you do not feel good about any action, take notice of that. It is usually is an indicator that you are not on the best course for you. Follow what gives you a good gut feeling, and when you get a strong impulse to act then be guided by your intuition and 'go for it'.

Join The Pro-'s. Forget The Anti-'s; Support What You Want To See In Your World

What are you against?
What you resist, persists (anything socially, globally, work, children, partner, friends)
Take your attention away from the things you do not want to see in your life, your environment, your community, society, the world. Turn your thoughts and your energy towards that which you want to see. The unconscious mind does not process negatives, so if you continue to think about the undesired elements you are fuelling them and creating more of the same.
Use your anti-list to create a pro-list.

Examples:

Personal Life
Anti: My husband isn't romantic.
Pro: I enjoy finding new ways to bring romance into our relationship.
Anti: My children are untidy.
Pro: I encourage and praise my children when they are helpful.
Anti: My friends aren't supportive.
Pro: I support my friends.
Anti: My family don't understand me.
Pro: I find ways to improve communication with my family.

Work
Anti: I don't feel valued.
Pro: I show appreciation for the work of others.
Anti: My colleagues are lazy.
Pro: I enjoy contributing to being part of a good team.

Community

Anti: I hate to see litter.
Pro: I take part in campaigns to clean up the environment.

Social

Anti: Young people round here are a problem.
Pro: I support local projects to help Young People.

Global

Anti: War is destructive
Pro: I promote Peace.
Anti: Poverty is distressing.
Pro: I find ways to help alleviate poverty.

Once you have your Pro-List, just focussing on what you want will bring positive change. And your Pro-List is a good starting point for asking yourself, "What am I going to do about it?

Some good Pro-words: *pro-active, propose, project, promise, progress, provide, protect, promote, proliferate, profess, process, produce, proceed, proclaim, prowess, profit, propitious, prospect*

10
Outcomes

Your Happy Story: Create A Metaphor For The Life You Want

You can write the script of the kind of life you want, which is a powerful process to help you create the kind of relationships, life-style, career, financial status and level of well-being and health you would like to enjoy in your life. By using metaphors to represent aspects of you, the hero or heroine of your own Happy Story, Success Story, Love Story or Whatever-You- Want-To-Call-It Story, you bypass the conscious mind, which can throw up all kinds of limiting thoughts and distractions, and directly address your unconscious mind. Metaphors are the language of the unconscious mind and the symbols we use to interpret and imbue our experiences with meaning, so your unconscious mind is taking on the meaning and purpose of what you intend, and will find a way to bring that into reality for you. Your unconscious mind has access to a far, far greater pool of knowledge, understanding and information than your conscious mind can ever grasp rationally. It is said to be teleological in nature, goal-orientated, and always knows the fastest and most effective route, albeit not always one you might anticipate, to achieving whatever it is you clearly intend.

So, it is an important step to first of all decide what exactly you want in your life, why you want it, and how it will benefit not only you, but people around you, and your environment. Once your intentions are very clear and compelling to you, you can create metaphors to represent them.

Your New, Happy Life-Story

Write down headings for different aspects of your life, such as Partner, Family, Friends, Career, Life-style, Money, Health. Make notes under each heading, detailing how you would like those to be. Get a picture in your mind of how you want the story to 'turn out' for each area, the 'Happy Ending', and feel how good those outcomes will feel. What will people be doing/saying? Where will you be?

Give your story a title.

Think of where you are now in your life. This will be the beginning.

Choose metaphors which are attractive to you for the characters, setting, action. These can be anything you like as long as they hold meaning for you, and the relationship between the characters represents your real relationships, e.g. spouse, children, family, friends, boss, colleagues.

Think of the dialogue; what significant things will the characters say, at key points in the story?

Plan the main events which will take you, the hero/heroine of your own life, from the beginning to a successful conclusion.

Give your characters the words, qualities and resources, such as special powers, weapons and things, which will enable them to achieve that end. These can be magical or otherwise, providing they are metaphors which represent to you a means of reaching the happy ending. (For example, the ability to fly may symbolise freedom or rising above conflict and obstacles; climbing a mountain may signify overcoming difficulties, persevering and success.

Have fun with your story, enjoy telling it to yourself when you are in a relaxed and receptive state, celebrate the realisation of it, and when this story becomes your reality, write an even more wonderful one for yourself. And remember that every good story has adventures and challenges to overcome, and every hero and heroine worth their salt triumph over the difficulties thrown in their way, in the end!